LET'S COOK WITH
Apples!

Delicious & Fun Apple Dishes Kids Can Make

Nancy Tuminelly

Consulting Editor, Diane Craig, M.A./Reading Specialist

A Division of ABDO

ABDO
Publishing Company

visit us at www.abdopublishing.com

Published by ABDO Publishing Company, a division of ABDO, P.O. Box 398166, Minneapolis, Minnesota 55439.
Copyright © 2013 by Abdo Consulting Group, Inc. International copyrights reserved in all countries. No part of this book may be reproduced in any form without written permission from the publisher. Super SandCastle™ is a trademark and logo of ABDO Publishing Company.

Printed in the United States of America, North Mankato, Minnesota
062012
092012

 PRINTED ON RECYCLED PAPER

Editor: Liz Salzmann
Content Developer: Nancy Tuminelly
Cover and Interior Design and Production: Colleen Dolphin, Mighty Media, Inc.
Food Production: Desirée Bussiere
Photo Credits: Colleen Dolphin, Shutterstock, iStockphoto (Gary Milner, Dawna Stafford)

The following manufacturers/names appearing in this book are trademarks: C&H® Pure Cane Sugar, Gold Medal® All-Purpose Flour, Heinz® Cider Vinegar, Karo® Light Corn Syrup, Kemps® Vanilla Frozen Yogurt, Morton's® Iodized Salt, Proctor Silex® Hand Blender, Old El Paso® Green Chilies, Pyrex® Measuring Glass, Roundy's® Cream Cheese, Roundy's® Orange Marmalade, Roundy's® Strawberry Preserves

Library of Congress Cataloging-in-Publication Data
Tuminelly, Nancy, 1952-
  Let's cook with apples! : delicious & fun apple dishes kids can make / Nancy Tuminelly.
    p. cm. -- (Super simple recipes)
  ISBN 978-1-61783-418-9
  1. Cooking (Apples)--Juvenile literature. 2. Apples--Juvenile literature. I. Title.
  TX813.A6T86 2013
  641.6'411--dc23

                    2011052133

Super SandCastle™ books are created by a team of professional educators, reading specialists, and content developers around five essential components—phonemic awareness, phonics, vocabulary, text comprehension, and fluency—to assist young readers as they develop reading skills and strategies and increase their general knowledge. All books are written, reviewed, and leveled for guided reading, early reading intervention, and Accelerated Reader® programs for use in shared, guided, and independent reading and writing activities to support a balanced approach to literacy instruction.

Note to Adult Helpers

Helping kids learn how to cook is fun! It's a great way to practice math and science. Cooking teaches kids about responsibility and boosts their confidence. Plus, they learn how to help out in the kitchen! The recipes in this book require adult assistance. Make sure there is always an adult around when kids are in the kitchen. Expect kids to make a mess, but also expect them to clean up after themselves. Most importantly, make the experience pleasurable by sharing and enjoying the food kids make.

Symbols

Knife
Always ask an adult to help you use knives.

Microwave
Be careful with hot food! Learn more on page 7.

Oven
Have an adult help put things into and take them out of the oven. Learn more on page 7.

Stovetop
Be careful around hot burners! Learn more on page 7.

Nuts
Some people can get very sick if they eat nuts.

Contents

Let's Cook with Apples!

Apples taste good and are good for you!
Apples can be eaten fresh or cooked.
They are a great snack anytime.

People have been eating apples for over
4,000 years! The **Pilgrims** brought apples
to America in 1620. Now the United States
grows one-third of the world's apples.

There are more than 7,000 kinds of
apples. Some are better for cooking.
Others are better for eating.

The recipes in this book are
simple. It's fun using one main
ingredient! Cooking teaches
you about food, measuring, and
following directions. Enjoy your
tasty treats with your family and
friends!

Think Safety!

- Ask an adult to help you use knives. Use a cutting board.

- Clean up spills to prevent accidents.

- Keep tools and **utensils** away from the edge of the table or counter.

- Use a step stool if you cannot reach something.

- Tie back long hair or wear a hat.

- Don't wear loose clothes. Roll up long **sleeves**.

- Keep a fire extinguisher in the cooking area.

Cooking Basics

Before you start...

- Get **permission** from an adult.

- Wash your hands.

- Read the recipe at least once.

- Set out all the ingredients and tools you will need.

When you're done...

- Cover food with plastic wrap or aluminum foil. Use **containers** with lids if you have them.

- Wash all of the dishes and **utensils**.

- Put all of the ingredients and tools back where you found them.

- Clean up your work space.

Using the Microwave

- Use microwave-safe dishes.

- Never put aluminum foil or metal in the microwave.

- Start with a short cook time. If it's not enough, cook it some more.

- Use oven mitts when taking things out of the microwave.

- Stop the microwave to stir liquids during heating.

Using the Stovetop

- Turn pot handles away from the burners and the edge of the stove.

- Use the temperature setting in the recipe.

- Use pot holders to handle hot pots and pans.

- Do not leave metal **utensils** in pots.

- Don't put anything except pots and pans on or near the burners.

- Use a timer. Check the food and cook it more if needed.

Using the Oven

- Use the temperature setting in the recipe.

- Preheat the oven while making the recipe.

- Use oven-safe dishes.

- Use pot holders or oven mitts to handle baking sheets and dishes.

- Do not touch oven doors. They can be very hot.

- Set a timer. Check the food and bake it more if needed.

A microwave, stovetop, and oven are very useful for cooking food. But they can be **dangerous** if you are not careful. Always ask an adult for help.

Measuring

Wet Ingredients

Set a measuring cup on the counter. Add the liquid until it reaches the amount you need. Check the measurement from eye level.

Dry Ingredients

Use a spoon to put the dry ingredient in the measuring cup or spoon. Put more than you need in the measuring cup or spoon. Run the back of a dinner knife across the top. This removes the extra.

Moist Ingredients

Moist ingredients are things such as brown sugar and dried fruit. They need to be packed down into the measuring cup. Keep packing until the ingredient reaches the measurement line.

Do You Know This = That?

There are different ways to measure the same amount.

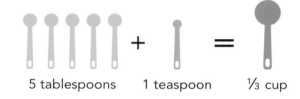

3 teaspoons	1 tablespoon		
4 tablespoons	¼ cup		
5 tablespoons	1 teaspoon	⅓ cup	

  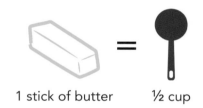

16 tablespoons = 1 cup

1 cup = 8 ounces

1 stick of butter = ½ cup

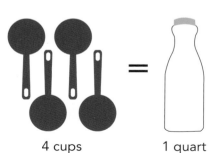 

2 cups = 1 pint

4 cups = 1 quart

2 quarts = ½ gallon

Cooking Terms

Mix
Combine ingredients with a mixing spoon. *Stir* is another word for mix.

Chop
Cut something into very small pieces with a knife.

Mash
Crush food until it is soft.

Core
Remove the center.

Peel
Remove skin from a fruit or vegetable. Use a peeler if needed.

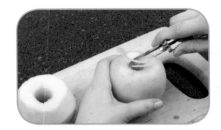

Slice
Cut something into thin pieces with a knife.

Boil
Heat liquid until it begins to bubble.

Chill
Put something in the refrigerator for a while.

What Kind of Apples to Use

Use **tart** apples for cooking. Sweet apples are best to eat fresh. Choose apples that are firm. They should have no **bruises** or soft spots. Always wash apples under running water before eating or cooking them. Dry them with a clean **towel**. Keep apples in an open plastic bag in the refrigerator.

Gala
(eating or cooking)

Golden Delicious
(eating, cooking, or pies)

Red Delicious
(eating)

Rome Beauty
(baking or drying)

Braeburn
(eating or cooking)

Granny Smith
(eating, cooking, or pies)

Tools

sharp knife

9 × 13-inch baking sheet

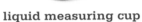

liquid measuring cup

dinner knife

mixing spoon

cutting board

rolling pin

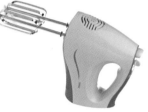

hand mixer

candy thermometer

pastry brush

oven mitts

timer

peeler & corer

plastic wrap

dry measuring cups

measuring spoons

glass baking dish

mixing bowl

aluminum foil

serving bowls

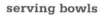

wooden craft sticks

can opener

pot holders

wax paper

small glass jars
with lids

paper plate

spatula

container with lid

paper towels

medium pot
with lid

ice cream scoop

dinner plate

ruler

large pot

Ingredients

cream cheese

assorted apples

powdered sugar

eggs

cinnamon red hot candies

tortilla chips

salt

cinnamon raisin bread

apple juice

cider vinegar

lemon juice

butter

green chilies

green onions

vanilla frozen yogurt

all-purpose flour

light corn syrup

orange
marmalade

fruit
preserves

golden raisins

raisins

brown sugar

chopped nuts

ground cumin

ginger root

sugar

peanuts

allspice

cinnamon sticks

coarse salt

ground cinnamon

pickling spice

granola

Awesome Apple-wich

A tasty sandwich that's good for you!

Makes 2 sandwiches

ingredients

1 cup cream cheese, softened

¼ cup unsalted peanuts, chopped

1 apple

1 teaspoon lemon juice

4 slices cinnamon raisin bread

tools

peeler & corer

dry measuring cups

mixing bowl

mixing spoon

sharp knife

cutting board

dinner knife

plastic wrap

1   Mix cream cheese and nuts in a bowl.

2   Core and peel the apple. Cut it into thin slices. Sprinkle lemon juice on the apple slices. This keeps them from turning brown.

3   Spread cheese and nut mixture on all four slices of bread.

4   Cover two of the bread slices with apples.

5   Put the other bread slices on top of the slices with apples.

6   Wrap the **sandwiches** in plastic wrap. Chill them in the refrigerator until you're ready to eat them.

Yummy Apple Sundaes

A fabulous fruity frozen dessert everyone will love!

Makes 6 servings

ingredients

6 large apples, cored, peeled, and cubed

1 cup golden raisins

⅔ cup apple juice

2 tablespoons sugar

2 teaspoons ground cinnamon

⅛ teaspoon allspice

vanilla frozen yogurt

granola

tools

peeler & corer

sharp knife

cutting board

measuring cups

measuring spoons

mixing spoon

medium pot with lid

pot holders

timer

serving bowls

ice cream scoop

1   Mix apples, raisins, apple juice, sugar, cinnamon, and allspice in a medium pot. Cover the pot.

2   Cook over medium heat until apples are soft. Stir often.

3   Remove from heat. Let stand 5 minutes. Mash apples slightly using the back of the mixing spoon.

4   Put two scoops of frozen yogurt in each serving bowl. Put some hot apple mixture on the frozen yogurt. Sprinkle granola on top. Eat right away!

Apple-icious Pickles

A sweet surprise for lunch, a snack, or anytime!

Makes 1 quart

ingredients

1 cup water
½ cup cider vinegar
½ cup sugar
2 slices ginger root
½ teaspoon course salt
1 teaspoon pickling spice
2 large red apples

tools

medium pot
mixing spoon
measuring cups
timer
pot holders
peeler & corer
sharp knife
cutting board
measuring spoons
3 small glass jars with lids
wax paper

1   Mix water, vinegar, and sugar in a medium pot. Cook over medium heat until the sugar **dissolves**. Cook for 5 more minutes. Remove from heat. Add ginger root, salt, and pickling spice.

2   Core the apples. Cut them lengthwise into quarters. Cut each piece in half again. Put the apples in the jars.

3   Pour the hot mixture into a liquid measuring cup. Then pour enough into each jar to cover the apples.

4   Fold pieces of wax paper to fit in the tops of the jars. Place one in each jar. Put the lids on the jars.

5   Put the jars in the refrigerator. Wait at least one hour before eating the apples. Eat them within three days.

Crispy Apple Chips

Wonderful with sandwiches or by themselves!

Makes 2 to 4 servings

ingredients
2 cups apple juice
1 cinnamon stick
2 large red apples, cored

tools
peeler & corer
large pot
measuring cups
sharp knife
cutting board
timer
spatula
paper towels
9 × 13-inch baking sheet
oven mitts
container with a lid

1   Preheat oven to 250 **degrees**. Put the apple juice and cinnamon stick in a large pot. Bring to a boil over medium-high heat.

2   Slice ½ inch (1 cm) off the top and bottom of each apple. Cut the apples crosswise into ⅛-inch (.3 cm) slices. Turn the apples as you slice them.

3   Put the apple slices in the boiling juice. Cook for 4 to 5 minutes.

4   Use a spatula to remove the apple slices. Pat them dry with a paper **towel**.

5   Put the slices on the baking sheet. Bake for 30 to 40 minutes. They should be slightly brown. Remove them from the oven. Let them cool completely. Store them in a **container** with a lid.

Sassy Apple Salsa

A scrumptious change from tomato salsa!

Makes 3 cups

ingredients

3 medium apples, cored
   and chopped
2 4-ounce cans green chilies,
   diced
½ cup raisins
½ cup green onions, sliced
⅓ cup cider vinegar
3 tablespoons brown sugar
¼ teaspoon ground cumin
   (optional)

tools

peeler & corer
can opener
mixing bowl
sharp knife
cutting board
measuring
cups

measuring
spoons
mixing spoon
plastic wrap
serving bowl

1 Mix apples, chilies, raisins, onions, vinegar, sugar, and cumin in a bowl.

2 Cover with plastic wrap. Chill for one hour.

3 Put in a serving bowl. Serve with tortilla chips.

TIP: Put shredded cheddar cheese on the chips. Heat in the microwave until the cheese melts.

Red Hot Candy Apples

Delicious dipped apples for a super special treat!

Makes 8 candied apples

ingredients

2 cups light corn syrup

1 cup sugar

½ cup cinnamon
red hot candies

8 medium red apples
with craft sticks
stuck into them

chopped nuts

tools

medium pot with lid

measuring cups

mixing spoon

timer

candy thermometer

wooden craft sticks

pot holders

paper plate

aluminum foil

1 Put corn syrup, sugar, and red hot candies in medium pot. Cook over medium-high heat. Stir constantly.

2 Cover the pot when the mixture starts boiling. Boil for 3 minutes.

3 Put the candy thermometer in the mixture. Keep cooking until the mixture is 290 **degrees**.

4 Remove the pot from the heat. Wait 2 minutes. Dip the apples in the mixture.

5 Put the nuts on a paper plate. Roll the apples in the nuts. Place the apples on aluminum foil to cool.

TIP: Spray the aluminum foil with cooking spray before placing the apples on it.

Fruity Baked Apples

A delightful, quick and easy apple snack or side dish!

Makes 2 servings

ingredients

2 large yellow apples, cored
jar of fruit preserves
4 tablespoons apple juice

tools

peeler & corer
glass baking dish
measuring spoons
microwave-safe plastic wrap
oven mitts
serving bowls

1   Peel the top third of each apple.

2   Place apples in a glass baking dish. Fill the center of each apple with fruit preserves.

3   Pour juice into the bottom of the dish. Cover with microwave-safe plastic wrap.

4   Microwave on high power for 5 to 6 minutes. The apples should be soft.

5   Put the apples in serving bowls. Be careful! They will be hot.

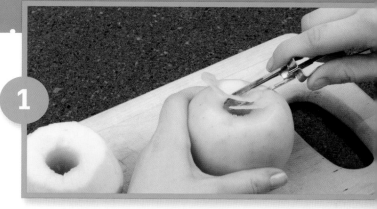

Terrific Apple Tartlets

Marvelous mini fruit pies perfect for a snack or dessert!

Makes 9 tartlets

ingredients

⅓ cup butter, softened

¼ cup powdered sugar

1 large egg

⅛ teaspoon salt

1⅓ cups all-purpose flour

1 large green apple, peeled, cored, and sliced

4 teaspoons orange marmalade

4 teaspoons sugar

tools

mixing bowl

measuring cups

measuring spoons

hand mixer

rolling pin

ruler

peeler & corer

9 × 13-inch baking sheet

sharp knife

cutting board

pastry brush

oven mitts

timer

1 Preheat oven to 375 **degrees**. Put the butter and powdered sugar in a mixing bowl. Beat with a hand mixer. Beat in egg and salt. Add the flour a little at a time. Mix it in with your hands.

2 Put the **dough** on a lightly floured surface. Roll it into a 9-inch (23 cm) square.

3 Cut the dough into nine squares. Put them on the baking sheet.

4 Pinch the sides of the squares up ¼ inch (1 cm) all the way around.

5 Put apple slices on each square. Brush marmalade on top of the apples. Sprinkle sugar over each square. Bake for 20 to 25 minutes.

Glossary

bruise – a soft, dark spot on a piece of fruit.

container – something that other things can be put into.

dangerous – able or likely to cause harm or injury.

degree – the unit used to measure temperature.

dissolve – to become part of a liquid.

dough – a thick mixture of flour, water, and other ingredients used in baking.

permission – when a person in charge says it's okay to do something.

Pilgrims – a group of people who came from England to America in the 1600s.

sandwich – two pieces of bread with a filling, such as meat, cheese, or peanut butter, between them.

sleeve – the part of a piece of clothing that covers some or all of the arm.

tart – having a sharp, sour taste.

towel – a cloth or paper used for cleaning or drying.

utensil – a tool used to prepare or eat food.